AUSTRALIA WIDE

SPIRIT OF A NATION

A Kevin Weldon Production
Published by Weldon Publishing
a division of Kevin Weldon & Associates
Pty Limited
372 Eastern Valley Way, Willoughby,
NSW 2068, Australia

First published 1991

Editor: Robert Coupe
Designer: Warren Penney
Typeset in Weiss by Savage Type Pty Ltd,
Queensland
Produced in Hong Kong by Mandarin Offset

National Library of Australia Cataloguing-in-
Publication data

Duncan Ken.
    Australia wide: spirit of a nation.
    Includes index.
    ISBN 1 86302 159 0.
    1. Australia—Description and travel—1990–
        —Views.
    1. Title.
994.0630222

Many of the images
displayed in this book are
available as signed limited-
edition Cibachrome prints.

For further information,
contact Ken Duncan
Australia Wide Gallery,
5740 Oak Road, Matcham,
New South Wales 2250,
AUSTRALIA.
Telephone: 61 43 67 6777

Endpapers: Cockburn Range,
near Wyndham, Western
Australia.

Page 1: Broken Falls, the
Grampians, Victoria.

Pages 2–3: Cape Leveque,
Western Australia.

Page 5: King Edward River,
Mitchell Plateau, Western
Australia.

Page 6: Bread Knife, Grand
High Tops, Warrumbungle
National Park, New South
Wales.

Page 7: River gum, Murray
River, Robinvale, Victoria.

ACKNOWLEDGMENTS

Our journey through life is filled with many encounters which help form the people we are. So it is with this book, and I thank all those who have helped in so many different ways to bring this visual diary to fruition.

Worthy of special note is my wife, Pamela, the unsung heroine, without whose many talents and support this project may never have come to pass.

I thank also the sponsors listed below. They are companies I have dealt with over several years and are each the best in their respective fields. KEN DUNCAN

This book is dedicated to a friend who died and rose again that we may have life in Him. His name is Jesus.

AUSTRALIA WIDE

SPIRIT OF A NATION

KEN DUNCAN

WELDON
PUBLISHING
SYDNEY · LONDON

CONTENTS

INTRODUCTION

I love the beauty and splendour of our nation. From early times, they have had a remarkable effect on people. The first mention of Australia in European recorded history was by the explorer who named it *Tierra Austrialia del Espiritu Santo* — "The Great South Land of the Holy Spirit". That Spirit is still in Australia today, and its presence is felt by residents and visitors alike; indeed, by all who seek out the country's prodigious natural treasures.

Australia is a land of dynamic contrasts which make us look beyond the natural to contemplate the magnificence of creation. Geologically, Australia is graced with some of the oldest formations on earth. Many theories, from slithering snakes to drifting land masses, have been presented to explain its origins, but most fail to pacify our questing spirit.

Our search for knowledge and understanding can be a barrier to the simple appreciation of beauty. A child is content to observe a butterfly in nature: to enjoy its erratic fluttering, its beautifully coloured wings as they sparkle in the sunlight. The seeker after knowledge feels the need to capture it, pin it to a board and classify it. The colour is still there, somewhat dulled perhaps, but the magic has gone. In our pursuit of worldly wisdom, we can easily lose our ability simply to walk in faith, in touch with the beauty with which God has surrounded us. With all our knowledge, what have we done for this beautiful planet?

Human knowledge will pass away, but the spirit within each person is eternal. Our country, too, has a spirit, and it could be a powerful unifying force, helping black and white to live and work harmoniously together. If only we could see ourselves as one people together in one nation, and look beyond mere self, we might be able to achieve real and lasting changes for the better. We can learn from the mistakes of other nations, rather than merely repeat them.

In this book I would like to share with you a journey of discovery. It is a journey that bypasses cities and takes you directly to the very heart of our land. Not everyone will have the opportunity to visit all the places described and photographed. However, in showing you some of the places that are special to me, I hope to instil in you a greater awareness of what I believe makes Australia unique—the Spirit of the Nation.

Above: Sand dunes at Myall Lakes National Park, New South Wales.

Overleaf: Cudmirrah Beach, New South Wales.

THE NORTH

Ranging from tropical rainforest to barren desert-like landscapes, the north of Australia is an area of great diversity which contains some of the oldest geological formations on earth—some of them within driving distance of large, modern towns and cities.

The weather in this part of the continent is affected by monsoons, and there are only two distinct seasons: the Wet and the Dry. During the Dry, the sun shines every day out of clear blue skies and the temperature settles on a constant, and comfortably warm, 32°C (90°F)—no need for weather forecasters in this season. In startling contrast, the Wet is often characterized by raging rivers, which can rise up to cover roads and bridges, making travel difficult and hazardous. Tropical cyclones are fairly common; some of them have been devastating. The most notorious and destructive of them all was Cyclone Tracy, which hit Darwin early on Christmas morning in 1975, virtually wiping out the city. Today, Darwin is once again a thriving city, bigger and better than before and showing few signs of the dreadful battering it took. It is a living proof of the resilience of its people.

What makes the Top End so special for me are the memories of the people I have met there and the adventures I shared with them. Life in the far north is typically uncomplicated, and issues are seen in fairly simple terms. Living far away from the nation's big cities, many of these people resent the fact that their lives are profoundly affected by the decisions of bureaucrats who often have no understanding of life on the land. As one of the oldest property owners in the Kimberley area of Western Australia said to me, "If only those guys down south would get on with the job of running the country rather than continually making new laws and rules and trying to run our lives, we'd all be better off." Perhaps it would be a good idea if our politicians were required to "go bush" for a few months with some of these locals. It might help them to get back in touch with what the real Australia is all about, and teach them that it really is OK to be Australian. It might also teach them to frame their laws to suit Australian conditions and not to try to make us like the rest of the world.

This was my first trip into this area, and my meetings and conversations with the locals certainly opened up for me new ways of looking at the world. It was a journey that genuinely changed my life and my way of thinking.

Left: Giant anthills at Turkey Creek, in the north-eastern corner of Western Australia.

THE JOURNEY

The Old Fella has passed away now. I call him "The Old Fella" out of respect, for it is a custom of the Aboriginal people not to mention a person by name after their death.

I first met The Old Fella in Derby, which was the launching point for an expedition that I was undertaking with my father and our dear friend Howard into a remote region of the Kimberley. The Old Fella was a full-blood Aborigine, an elder of his tribe, who had lived in the area we were to explore some 25 years earlier. My father and Howard had first known him in the time before Aboriginal people were taken from their tribal lands and placed in settlements.

With our four-wheel drive loaded with fuel, supplies and camera equipment, we made our first stop at Mt Elizabeth Station. From there we had to force a track to the abandoned Pantijana Station, more than 200 kilometres (125 miles) to the north. Here the formidable terrain blocked our path, so we were forced to leave the vehicle and continue on foot.

We carried some basic rations but, in order to keep our packs as light as possible, intended to live mainly off the land. Dad and Howard began studying their survey map to decide how best to access an area that Howard had last visited 25 years earlier. The Old Fella was bewildered at the white man's attempt to plot a course by looking at lines and squiggles on a piece of paper. When, however, they had finally decided on a course, The Old Fella nodded in agreement — just to get the journey under way.

As there are few outstanding landmarks in this region on which to get a bearing, we kept as straight a course as possible. It was hard slog through wild country, and so intent were we on reaching our destination that the journey itself became an affliction. To make matters worse, The Old Fella kept falling behind, as if he were being dragged away from an old friend.

On the fourth day, we were standing on the crest of a hill trying to get our bearings for the next stage, when The Old Fella finally spoke up. "You show me what you're aiming for. I'll meet you there and find some bush tucker on the way," he said. When we got to our next destination, The Old Fella was already there, holding some lily roots he had gathered. In contrast to us stubborn white fellas, who dumped our packs in sheer exhaustion, he looked relaxed and refreshed. From that point on, we decided to follow The Old Fella's lead. Although we kept to our schedule, the whole journey had changed in character — from an effort into an adventure. It was like walking through nature's supermarket as we watched The Old Fella gather all kinds of different foods along the way. My favourite was bush honey.

After a week of travelling, however, I began to feel restless and impatient to get to our destination. I asked The Old Fella how far we had still to go. He answered, "Little bit long way, maybe one jump-up, maybe two." (A jump-up was his term for a hill.) By midday the next day we still had not got there and I asked again, "How much further?" He gave me the standard reply, "Little bit long way." Barely curbing my anger and frustration, I walked on. The next day I asked for the last time, "OK, Old Fella, how much further?" His predictable reply was delivered right on cue. "That's it," I exploded. "I want to know exactly how far we still have to go." He looked at me with soft eyes and said, "Does it really matter how far, or when? Shouldn't the journey be as important as the destination?" Talk about a man of few words! What could I say? He was right, of course. I had been so obsessed with reaching a particular place that I was failing to appreciate the journey.

We did finally arrive, and we made some great discoveries. But these were secondary to the lesson I had learned from The Old Fella: the journey should always be as important as the destination. If you don't enjoy the journey, is there any point in getting to your destination? It is, after all, the journey that gives the destination its real meaning.

Overleaf: King George Falls, Western Australia. The King George River plummets 60 metres (200 feet) to sea level. The deep, dark water in the gorge is surrounded by cliffs of rich ochre which dwarf the trees in the surrounding landscape.

The Whitsunday group of islands, off the coast of Queensland, forms the gateway to the fabulous Great Barrier Reef. Here we see Hill Inlet, on Whitsunday Island, the largest island of the group and a veritable Pacific paradise.

Above: The frilled lizard, one of Australia's most distinctive reptiles, is a common sight throughout northern Australia.

Right: Situated not far from the West Australian town of Derby, Mt Barnett Station, in the Manning Gorge, is a cattle station that is owned and run by Aborigines. What better way to relax after a hard day's work than to contemplate twilight reflections in the still water?

Overleaf: When the wet season brings the first rains in many months, this dried-up creekbed in the Bungle Bungles will be transformed into a swiftly flowing stream.

The Drysdale River, a ribbon of life in an arid landscape, flows through the
Kimberley in Western Australia until it plunges over the Drysdale Falls. Water
is the most valuable, and often the scarcest, of all resources in Australia's dry
outback regions.

Above: The Roe River, in the Kimberley, forms part of a remote and spectacular wilderness.

Overleaf: Fires, most of them deliberately lit, are a familiar sight during the dry season in the Top End. The practice of burning off, begun in ancient times by Aborigines, is still carried on by modern farmers, who understand the benefits of clearing out the old growth to make way for the lush new shoots.

Above: Palm fronds, at Mataranka, about 100 kilometres (60 miles) south-east of Katherine in the Northern Territory.

Left: The early evening light enhances the rich ochres in the cliffs at Cape Leveque in the Kimberley.

Overleaf: Like most of the Great Barrier Reef, Hardys Reef supports an abundance of jewel-like marine life. But, despite their alluring beauty, reefs such as this were a nightmare for early navigators, who had to find a passage through them without the aid of charts.

Right: A full moon rises over Western Australia's Bungle Bungles, its soft, caressing light enhancing the subtleties of colour and texture that are highlighted by the golden afterglow of the dying sun.

Below: The Magnificent Gallery at Laura, in northern Queensland. The area around Laura is rich in Aboriginal rock paintings.

Above: Tomato, a beer-drinking steer, at Escott Station, north-west Queensland.

Left: Football is a tough sport at the best of times, but in mud football, where the game is played in a deep quagmire, the players flail about like primitive swamp creatures. These teams are doing battle with each other—and with the dreadful conditions—at Derby in Western Australia.

Overleaf: The incessant bubbling of the water, the soft rustle of the trees, the songs of birds carried gently on the breeze—all combine to create a great symphony of nature in this tranquil setting on the Mossman River in Queensland's Mossman Gorge.

These drinkers, in a public bar in Mt Garnet, Queensland, are watching a telecast
of a boxing match in which Jeff Fenech, one of Australia's sporting greats, is trying
to add yet another title to his list. As the customers watch their hero, the usual
noise and bustle of the bar are replaced by a mesmerized silence.

Above: This perfect example of an old-fashioned general store is at Croydon, in Queensland's Gulf Country. Stores such as this cater for all the shopping needs of the local residents—from basic foodstuffs all the way through to tractor parts.

Overleaf: Boundaries are so far apart on the long and dusty Kalumburu Road, in the Kimberley, that it is easy to forget you are travelling through private property. If you forget to close one of these gates, however, and the cattle get out, you will soon incur the wrath of the normally friendly locals.

Previous page: In Queensland's Mossman Gorge, a swimming hole, fashioned by nature and fringed by dense rainforest foliage, provides a welcome respite from the all-pervading heat and humidity.

Right: Bathurst Island is one of the islands that comprise the Tiwi group. These children, from Nguiu Settlement, delighted in first sinking our dinghy and then refloating it while we were buying supplies on their island.

Overleaf: In this early morning shot of the ancient Bungle Bungles in Western Australia's Kimberley region, masses of dome-shaped mounds rise dramatically from the desert floor. Over millions of years, erosion has sculpted the soft curves of these mountains and etched out features such as the arch that can be seen in the foreground.

Above: An Aboriginal boy at Mt Barnett Station in Western Australia's Kimberley region.

Left: Relieved to settle down for the night after a dusty day's travelling in the Kimberley, we camped for the night at Drysdale River Crossing.

Above: Staghorn ferns grow prolifically in Queensland's tropical and subtropical forests.

Left: The first rays of sunshine dissolve the darkness at the beginning of a new day to reveal the curtain-like foliage of this beautiful casuarina tree at Noahs Beach, Daintree, in northern Queensland.

Overleaf: The rhythmic lapping of the clear water on the shore imparts a feeling of tranquillity to this beach scene, north of Palm Cove in Queensland.

Left: Sunset reflections in the waters of the King Edward River in Western Australia's Kimberley region.

Below: Aboriginal rock painting, Kakadu, Northern Territory.

Above: Bark peels from the trunk of this gum tree in northern Queensland.

Right: The lacy curtain of the Millstream Falls, on Queensland's Atherton Tableland, forms the perfect backdrop to this spectacular natural amphitheatre.

Overleaf: Pandanus palms stand like silent sentinels at Cape Leveque, Western Australia—protectors of the land and reminiscent of its ancient landscape.

Above: A family at Mt Elizabeth Station in the Kimberley.

Left: Not many people would attempt to rebuild a motor under these conditions. However, these "bush mechanics", at Gibb River Road, Western Australia, were determined to get the vehicle mobile—and they eventually succeeded.

Left: A profound sense of serenity pervades this tropical rainforest scene, at Oliver Creek in Queensland's Daintree River National Park. A buttress tree occupies the foreground; in the background can be seen examples of the aptly named fan palm, a predominant species in some north Queensland rainforest areas.

Right: The Bell Creek Falls, on Silent Grove Station, Western Australia, take their name from the creek that joins the Isdell River just before it reaches the falls. Both these streams are spring-fed, and flow continuously throughout the year.

Overleaf: In this Kimberley landscape, near Derby, termites reign supreme. To the casual observer, the only sign of their presence is the flint-hard terracotta cathedrals that dot the countryside. Nothing here grows tall—except the hardy boab trees.

Above: The king parrot inhabits mountains and forests all along the eastern edge of the continent.

Left: This is the sixth of a series of gorges in the Northern Territory known collectively as the Katherine Gorge. Each gorge has its own distinctive character. This peaceful early morning scene was photographed during the dry season. At the beginning of the wet season the river is transformed into a raging torrent.

Overleaf: The stone cliffs of the north side of the Bungle Bungles dominate the surrounding Kimberley landscape, which is brilliantly brought to life in the golden late afternoon sunlight. Scattered eucalypts cast their lengthening shadows over the burnished sands, typically covered with clumps of spinifex.

Right: The simple and majestic beauty of Cape Leveque in the Kimberley in Western Australia conjures up a mood of peaceful repose which is in striking contrast to the complex, bustling and ever-changing world that most of us inhabit.

Overleaf: The water, reflecting the rich and sombre hues of the sky at sunset, gently laps the shoreline in this twilight scene at Cape Leveque in Western Australia.

THE CENTRE

When most people think of the "centre" of Australia, they conjure up an image of the arid outback — of a landscape dominated by the massive shape of Uluru, or Ayers Rock, or the towering domes of Mount Olga. For me, however, this notion is too limiting, focusing attention on what is, after all, only one among a great variety of scenes and landscapes that are all typically Australian.

In this book I have taken the "centre" to mean the central strip of the continent, from the predominantly warm subtropical areas towards the north to the temperate region, with more clearly differentiated seasonal variations, towards the south; from the heavily populated and fertile eastern coastal strip, through the often forbidding outback deserts, where one

would sometimes be hard pressed to find a dozen people within a radius of a hundred kilometres, to the rugged west coast with its rich wheatbelt and significant centres of population. It is by far the largest, in terms of area, of the three sections covered in this book, and undoubtedly the most diverse.

In spite of this, about three-quarters of this area could be classified as arid desert or semi-arid country. As well as the universally known and now reasonably accessible tourist attractions, there are many sites of outstanding beauty and unique character in what is often called the "dry heart" of the continent. And there are no doubt still some secrets which this alluring but harsh country has not yet yielded up. Many, venturing into this unfamiliar and uncompromising terrain, have perished in the attempt to uncover them. The legendary explorers Burke and Wills were two; closer to our times, in 1931, Harold Lasseter, seeking out the rich vein of gold that he remembered finding more than thirty years earlier, starved to death in the ancient and remote Petermann Ranges. The diary that he left behind vividly evokes for us the agonizing frustration of his fruitless search and the bitter anguish of his final days.

Lasseter's Reef remains one of the great enigmas of Australian folklore, the subject of numerous books and of much fanciful conjecturing. Its elusiveness and its fabled richness challenge the popular imagination. It may yet provide abundant rewards to some intrepid adventurer with the courage and dedication to rediscover it.

A GIFT

From Port Augusta in South Australia right up to Darwin in the Northern Territory there runs a road that is officially called the Stuart Highway. But to locals it is known simply as "The Track". It is a lifeline running through the centre of Australia. Towns—often hundreds of kilometres apart—are scattered along it. When asked for directions, the locals talk in terms of so many hundred kilometres up or down "The Track". The "centre" is always where you happen to be at any particular time.

It is not really a well-travelled road. In some places it is barely wide enough to accommodate a single vehicle, and the unseasoned outback tourist is confronted by numerous hazards, both natural and unnatural. Road trains probably represent the greatest danger. A road train is a large

truck which hauls two or three trailers full of cattle, food supplies or virtually any kind of goods over huge distances in the outback. When one of these thundering juggernauts comes hurtling towards you at 100 kilometres (60 miles) or more per hour, the wise driver will give it a wide berth. People who stick to the principle—admirable in theory—that all vehicles have equal rights on the road, are likely to end up decorating a road train's bull bar. "Might is right" is a much more appropriate dictum in this situation. When you see one of these monsters approaching—get off the road.

My first trip up "The Track" was about eight years ago, when I started my photographic journey. I still had a lot of city slicker in me then, and I was off in search of adventure and discovery. In

those days "The Track" was still a dirt road, and even more perilous than it is today. It was while travelling along this road, dodging road trains and avoiding treacherous potholes, as well as kangaroos and a variety of other wildlife, that I discovered an interesting custom of outback travellers. People invariably waved as they passed you on the road, a custom that, with my city background, I found rather strange at first. If you waved at everyone you passed in city traffic, you'd end up with your wrist permanently out of joint.

I think part of the reason for waving to strangers is that people find it reassuring to see another human being in the vastness of the outback; it makes them feel less alone, less vulnerable. It was not long before I began to enjoy the custom, and waved happily to all who passed. It sometimes landed me in difficulties—for example, when it was necessary to swerve to avoid a road train in the middle of my "Hi, have a great day!" wave. More than once I ended up sliding about precariously in loose gravel.

On the odd occasion people did not wave back, I found it disconcerting. I made excuses for them—maybe she didn't see me wave; maybe his reflexes were a bit slow. But even then, I felt cheated

when someone failed to return my wave. I realized that this feeling was irrational and I pondered the reason for it. Why, I asked myself, did it matter to me whether people waved or not? Then it occurred to me that I was waving, not simply to say hello, but because I wanted something in return.

This seemingly small insight has been of great benefit to me. It has made me understand that when we give of ourselves, we should do so spontaneously

Above: Waves, rolling in from the warm waters of the Coral Sea, break on Seventy-Five Mile Beach, the vast expanse of sand that stretches along much of the eastern coast of Fraser Island, off the coast of Queensland.

and without any thought of getting something in return. Greeting other people, even strangers, is an expression of affection, and love and affection should, like any gift, be given freely and unconditionally.

Overleaf: The sun's afterglow sheds a muted light on this lagoon at Davistown on the New South Wales Central Coast. On this classically still evening, every detail of the scene, including the luminescent hues of the evening sky, produces its perfect mirror image beneath the unruffled surface of the water.

Central Station, situated near the very centre of Fraser Island, off the coast of Queensland, is an area characterized by lush and towering forests. Here, at Pile Valley, a recent shower of rain has given an added lustre to the foliage and intensified the distinctive and refreshing odours of an Australian rainforest.

Above: Old farm ruins near Goomalling, north-east of Perth in Western Australia.

Left: The rough simplicity of this cane-cutter's cottage in the heart of Queensland's sugar country reflects the arduous conditions under which many of these workers lived and worked before the advent of mechanization.

Overleaf: The warm and radiant colours of Mount Olga, the wondrous conglomeration of massive stone domes to the west of Ayers Rock, are seen to wonderful effect in the first rays of the morning sun. This site is known to the Aborigines as Katajuta, which means "many heads". The shadow that falls at the base of the foremost dome was cast by the dome from which the photograph was taken.

Above: Early morning light illuminates these sand dunes on Fraser Island, Queensland.

Right: Here, near Waddy Point on the north-eastern coast of Fraser Island, is just one example of the many spectacular sand dunes that, with the wonderful perched lakes and the lush forests, constitute the major attractions of this island, the world's largest sandmass. The action of the sea and wind combine to form these dunes and to keep them in a state of constant change. Wind-borne particles of sand create the soft edge that is visible on the crest of this dune.

Left: A disused petrol bowser has been unceremoniously abandoned in the middle of the desert near Silverton in the extreme far west of New South Wales. Except for the mountain range in the far distance, this forlorn and now useless object provides the only relief from the flat monotony of this desolate landscape.

Overleaf: In this shot, looking north from Indian Head on the north-east coast of Fraser Island, the distinctive spiky and spiralling foliage of pandanus plants, which grow prolifically on the island, are visible in the foreground. Not surprisingly, they are often popularly called screw palms. Beneath the headland the emerald sea breaks on the long ribbon of white sand which stretches away to Waddy Point, the next headland.

The unique Lake Wabby is one of the glories of Fraser Island, but the forces
of nature that formed it are also working towards its demise. The extensive
sandblow which forms its eastern shoreline first created the lake when it dammed
up the waters of a creek; it is now, slowly but inexorably, encroaching upon it.

The north face of Uluru, with the famous "brain" formation seemingly etched
into the rock. The rich ochre colours of the rock face stand out in brilliant relief
against the deep blue of the midday sky. The eucalypt trees in the foreground
are dwarfed by the size and grandeur of the great monolith.

Left: A vivid symbol of human vulnerability, the broken wreck of the *Maheno*, victim of a cyclone in 1935, lies on a beach on the east coast of Fraser Island, its formerly imposing superstructure now all but disintegrated and its once watertight hull invaded by fish. When it was wrecked, the 30-year-old former trans-Tasman liner had already ended its sailing career and was being towed to Japan to be sold as scrap.

Overleaf: So wonderfully clear is the water in Wanggoolba Creek, at Central Station on Fraser Island, that, except for the reflections and the gentle swish of the flowing stream, it would be easy to imagine that one was looking at dry sand. This clarity is also deceptive, as it disguises the fact that, in some places, the water is about a metre (several feet) deep. The sand, the water and the verdant rainforest vegetation all combine to produce a scene that gladdens the spirit and reflects the quiet majesty of creation.

Above: A dingo at Indian Head on Fraser Island, Queensland.

Right: A rather scrawny eucalypt manages to thrive in the middle of the "Baby Marbles", one of the many outcrops of the so-called Devil's Marbles, south of Tennant Creek in the Northern Territory.

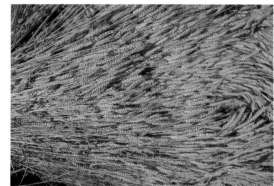

Above: Wheat stooks at Grass Valley in south-western Western Australia.

Left: Although Western Australia's wheatbelt is confined to the relatively fertile south-western section of the state — from south of Perth north as far as Geraldton — it accounts for a significant proportion of the nation's wheat production. Large amounts of other cereal crops, such as barley and oats, are also grown. This scene, at Spencer's Brook, north-west of Perth, is typical of the open, gently undulating landscapes in this area.

Overleaf: A lone figure strolls along Terrigal Beach, with its sheltered lagoon, on the Central Coast of New South Wales, no doubt savouring the quiet solitude that the approach of evening brings to this normally bustling place.

Left: The celebrated rock formation known as the Three Sisters rises impressively out of the Jamieson Valley, one of the world's greatest canyons, in the Blue Mountains, west of Sydney in New South Wales. The Blue Mountains form part of the Great Dividing Range, which stretches continuously almost the entire length of the continent near its eastern seaboard, forming a natural barrier between the heavily populated coastal fringe and the great inland plains. For almost a quarter of a century after the first European settlement, this barrier remained impenetrable to the new settlers.

Right: A salmon gum in a wheatfield at sunset, Goomalling, Western Australia.

Right: This classic, but now dilapidated, Queensland homestead, raised on its characteristic stilts, at Miriam Vale, about 450 kilometres (280 miles) north of Brisbane, was home to several generations of farmers and their families. It has now been abandoned for a more modern, but less distinctive, house. Like many local traditions, the famous "Queenslander" house is under increasing threat from the forces of uniformity.

Overleaf: This rare sunrise view of The Skillion, at Terrigal in New South Wales, was taken from a nearby rock platform. On many mornings cloud or mist, or a combination of both, diminishes the clarity of the sunlight as it is absorbed and reflected by the towering stone headland.

Right: The ancient volcanic formations of the Glasshouse Mountains, just inland from the coast, form a picturesque background to this small farm at Peachester, about 70 kilometres (45 miles) north of Brisbane. The brilliant purple-mauve blooms of a jacaranda tree dominate the centre foreground. Even though it is an introduced species, the jacaranda thrives along the east coast of Australia and is particularly prolific in subtropical environments.

Below: Fallen jacaranda blooms scattered on the ground. These beautiful trees grow abundantly in eastern Australia.

Left: Spread over a wide area about 100 kilometres (60 miles) south of Tennant Creek in the Northern Territory, these mighty boulders, each perched precariously on a tiny base, are generally referred to as the Devil's Marbles. I call them "God's Marbles" because to me these great natural sculptures, and their apparent defiance of the laws of gravity, are powerful symbols of the awesome majesty of creation.

Overleaf: The Skillion, the rocky headland at Terrigal, on the Central Coast of New South Wales, here assumes its sombre aspect, warning off those who would venture too near. The effect of a boiling sea raging impotently at the base of the cliff is enhanced by the short time exposure that was used to achieve this atmospheric shot, which I have named "Rising Force".

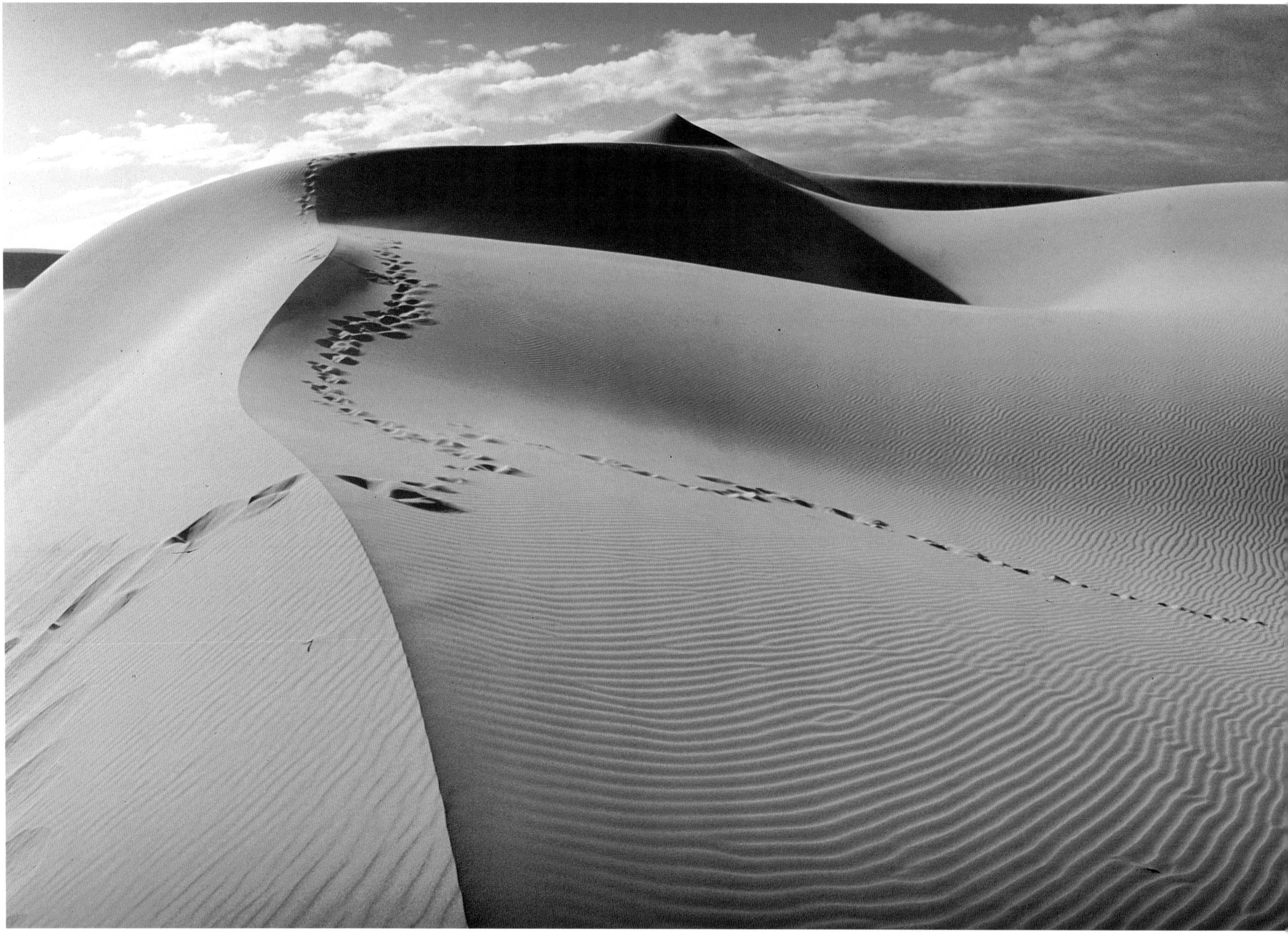

Left: From the 1870s until 1929 Eucla, on the southern coast of Western Australia, near its border with South Australia, was the site of a telegraph station on the overland telegraph line between Adelaide and Albany, south-east of Perth. Since then the sands, obeying the whims of the area's swirling winds, have built up into undulating dunes and completely covered many of the buildings that were once a vital part of a national communications network.

Below: A ghost gum stands out in stark relief against the balanced boulders of the so-called Devil's Marbles in the Northern Territory.

The swirling fins of the windmill provide the only hint of movement in this placid scene near Cunnamulla in south-western Queensland. The dying rays of the sun cast a similar golden glow on the small tree that grows beside the waterhole and on the vane of the windmill. Cunnamulla, an important wool centre, is an Aboriginal word meaning "big waterhole".

A sense of stillness, enhanced by the subtle pastel hues of the late afternoon sky,
pervades this scene in which a lone stockman surveys a herd of grazing cattle
near Scone in New South Wales' upper Hunter Valley. Scone is at the centre
of a rich and extensive pastoral and dairy area.

Right: A resplendent sunrise at Terrigal Beach, on the New South Wales Central Coast, its serenity tempered only by the dark clouds that are gathering near the horizon. Silhouetted on the left is Forresters Headland.

Overleaf: About 200 kilometres (125 miles) north of Perth in Western Australia is the Nambung National Park. Among the extensive sand dunes and scrubby vegetation in this area are the limestone formations known as the Pinnacles. Standing as high as 5 metres (16 feet), and moulded by time and weather into varied and often bizarre shapes, they are suggestive of a lunar landscape. They are thought by some scientists to be remnants of ancient forests which once flourished in this area.

Right: Dust from the unsealed road hangs in the air, imparting a softness to what is often considered a harsh and uncompromising landscape — a softness enhanced by the lingering rays of the sun, the drooping foliage of the desert oaks that line the road, and the full moon that rises over the top of Uluru, or Ayers Rock. The much-travelled road, which leads from Mount Olga to Ayers Rock, has since been sealed, increasing the comfort of tourists but detracting from the harmonious blending of colours that characterizes this scene.

Overleaf: The morning sun peeps over the horizon, its still gentle beams highlighting the undulations of the sand dunes and silhouetting Indian Head, one of the main landmarks on the north-eastern coast of Fraser Island. Indian Head, which is known to the Aborigines as *Walaar* (meaning "basalt"), was given its English name by Captain James Cook as he sailed up the east coast of the continent in 1770. He so named it because of the group of Aborigines who had gathered on the headland to watch the progress of the alien craft.

Previous page: An early morning shot of Lake Boomanjin, one of the more than forty "perched" lakes that are spread throughout Fraser Island. The melaleuca in the foreground, its distinctive "paper bark" highlighted by the morning sun, is but one of the many examples of this species that line this and most other Fraser Island lakes. The "black water" in which the tree is reflected is caused by tannin from leaves and other organic matter that finds its way into the lake.

Left: These reflections, in a large saltlake near the mining town of Kambalda in the south of Western Australia, evoke for me the concepts of earth and heaven. The dividing line between them is accentuated by the fine white line of salt which is visible in the far distance. The heavenly opalescence of the sky is reflected, but with diminished brilliance, in the earthbound waters of the lake.

Overleaf: Burning sugar cane to remove foliage and facilitate harvesting the crop is a time-honoured tradition in Queensland's sugar country, but one that is increasingly questioned by present-day farmers. It is claimed by many that burning off both reduces the plant's yield and deprives the soil of the nutrients and mulching benefits of the foliage. This cane fire was photographed at Cannonvale, in the coastal area north of the large town of Mackay.

Above: Reflections in Lake Boomanjin on Fraser Island.

Left: This aerial shot of Rainbow Beach, on the Queensland coast near Fraser Island, reveals the spectacularly variegated walls of sand that rise up from the beach front. The subtle gradations of colours, ranging from deep ochres to rich reds, are the result of iron oxides that have accumulated in the sand over many millennia and have been exposed by centuries of erosion. The beach here can be treacherous; sudden changes of tide have caught many a vehicle, and its occupants, unawares.

Overleaf: A sense of brooding is tempered by the delicate effects of filtered light in this sunset scene at Kambalda in Western Australia. In the centre, a shower of rain, borne by ominous-looking dark clouds, brings relief to the cracked and salt-encrusted lakebed, parched by days of searing heat. Because of the power and sense of movement inherent in this panorama, I have named the picture "Divine Motion".

THE SOUTH

Although it is smaller in area than the other two regions covered in this book, the south is the most densely populated part of our nation. Approximately 65 per cent of Australians live in the part of Australia that falls below a horizontal line drawn on the map from Sydney in the east to a point south of Perth on the west coast.

It is a region of well-defined seasons, where scorching summers can give way to very cold winters, and where in some alpine locations snow can blanket the ground for most of the year. It is also a region of diverse terrains, ranging from desert plains, through undulating hills and lush valleys, to spectacularly rugged mountain ranges.

For most of my life I have lived in the eastern corner of this southern section. Born in Mildura on the Murray River, I spent a good part of my early life in various country towns before moving, at the age of sixteen, to Sydney, the "big smoke". It proved to be a good move for me, for it opened up career opportunities and allowed me to discover the magic and excitement of photography.

It was in Sydney, while I was in my early twenties, that I first began to nurture the dream of returning to the bush to photograph the natural wonders, and the people, of this vast nation.

FOLLOWING OUR DREAMS

The Cradle Mountain–Lake St Clair National Park in Tasmania's central highlands is one of nature's great edifices. It is an area of sheer wilderness, characterized by soaring peaks, massive and evocative rock formations, wild and rugged valleys and idyllic and limpid alpine lakes. It is an area that arouses the spirit and challenges the sense of adventure that exists in all of us — a world away from the artificial environment, with its materialistic preoccupations and ambitions, in which

Left: The Twelve Apostles, at Port Campbell, Victoria, are being steadily eroded by the inexorable forces of wind and waves.

most of us live. It is not an area you can travel through in air-conditioned comfort; much of it is inaccessible except on foot, and the visitor to this region must be ever on the lookout for swift changes of weather which can bring sudden and treacherous snowdrifts.

It was while hiking in this wilderness, marvelling at its grandeur, that I was struck by the way in which supposedly comfortable urban lifestyles can sap our vital energies, dilute our natural hunger for adventure and divert us from realizing our most cherished dreams. As I slaked my thirst in the pure, cold water of the Twisted Lakes after hours of arduous trekking, and enjoyed its soothing refreshment, it suddenly occurred to me that many people, even those with a deep and genuine feel for the wilderness, would never know the joy of being in this wondrous place — or, indeed, in any similarly beautiful but remote area. It occurred to me, too, that they would be the poorer for having missed out on such an experience.

It is all too easy to spend one's life in search of the great materialistic dream, always maintaining that there is no time for real adventure, or that when there is time, the conditions are no longer right. These are often delusions. I have walked

hundreds of kilometres in the outback with a man seventy-three years young. I have spent time with a family with seven children, ranging in age from three months to thirteen years, who live on a Malayan *prau* and sail around Arnhem Land. They are people whose lives have been enriched and whose outlook has been broadened by their adventures.

I'm not suggesting that we should all become nomadic travellers, but I do believe we need a balance in our lives — a balance between normality and adventure; between our own comfort zones and being "stretched" a little. We need time away from our hectic day-to-day lives to sit back and see what is really happening. Nothing restores the world-weary soul quite like taking the time to contemplate the beauty and immensity of

creation. Whatever problems we may have will fall into perspective as we look up in wonder at the heavens, adorned by countless stars that are undimmed by city lights. Dreams will again seem possible as we sit mesmerized by the flames of a campfire. Hopes will be restored as we sit on a beach, gazing upon the endlessness of the ocean.

There is a power behind creation that is bigger than we are. How can anyone believe that creation revolves around themselves alone? As we look beyond our immediate circumstances and surroundings we will be buoyed by the realization that there is much more to existence than can be grasped by our limited human understanding. Faith is that which is hoped for, but not seen.

All our striving for money, power and position — the glittering prizes that society often holds up as ideals — counts for nothing in the end if our spirit remains unfulfilled. You can't take your Lego blocks with you: you must leave them on earth for others to play with. The only acquisition you can take with you is the spiritual wealth you have accumulated in your time on this planet. The spirit is eternal; the body is simply a tent that serves our purposes during our "camp" on earth.

Too often our response to possibilities for fulfilment is tempered by fear — fear of the unknown. Faith is the opposite of and the antidote to fear. Faith carries us forward, while fear holds us back, prisoners of our own minds. Faith that there is a purpose in creation that transcends self will nurture our spirit of adventure and allow us to follow, rather than shrink from, our dreams. There is only one life on earth that we know of, and we are living it right now. Let's make the most of the great adventure that it offers us.

Overleaf: As its name suggests, Refuge Cove, on the eastern side of Wilson's Promontory in Victoria, has long provided a sheltered haven for seafarers from the treacherous waters of Bass Strait. The limpid waters and clear skies here belie the fury of the storms which often lash this, the most southerly, part of the Australian continent.

Above: An orange willow at Deloraine, Tasmania.

Left: The Tarra-Bulga National Park is in the Strzelecki Ranges, south-east of the Victorian capital of Melbourne. It is an area of high rainfall, and this accounts for the superb fern gullies that abound in the parts of these mountains that have not been cleared for dairying, as well as the mists that often shroud the valleys. This shot was taken from the Grand Ridge Road, which runs through the park.

Right: Ancient glaciers forged the precipitous landscapes of the Cradle Mountain-Lake St Clair National Park in Tasmania's central highlands, creating such majestic and towering shapes as this "razorback" formation.

Overleaf: The denuded limbs of dead eucalypts reach out of the waters of the Lake Victoria reservoir in the south-western corner of New South Wales. The reservoir is supplied by means of an artificial channel from the Murray River.

The rolling hills of the Strzelecki Ranges were once thickly forested. Now largely stripped of their lush vegetation, they provide ideal grazing country for sheep and dairy cattle.

A prolonged dry spell has robbed these undulating hills, near Korumburra in
southern Victoria's Strzelecki Ranges, of the rich green which usually clothes
them. Their present brownish tones are accentuated by the warm light and the
opalescent hues of the late afternoon sky.

Right: As the camera pans skywards on a misty day in the Quamby Bluff Reserve in northern Tasmania, the foliage at the crowns of these soaring eucalypts takes on the appearance of a distant and delicate lacework pattern.

Overleaf: The late afternoon sun casts its warm glow over the rocky foreshores and thick heath vegetation of Freshwater Cove on Wilson's Promontory. The reddish patches visible in the granite rocks is a lichen that grows commonly on rocks in this area.

The Smiths have a monopoly on the retail trade in the tiny community of Bagdad, about 30 kilometres (20 miles) north of Hobart, the Tasmanian capital. Their neatly picturesque general store, with its wide verandah and decorative wrought iron, caters for all the locals' needs, from food to fuel.

Left: This huddled conglomeration of vertical and slanting pencil-like boulders stands at the summit of Mt Wellington, the peak that dominates Hobart, in south-eastern Tasmania. It has been dubbed, rather fancifully, the Organ Pipes.

Overleaf: In this atmospheric view from the Grand Ridge Road in Victoria's Strzelecki Ranges the foreground is dominated by the lush tree ferns that proliferate in these moist valleys, while in the distance the vegetation merges gently into the all-pervading greyness of the mist.

Right: During the non-shearing season quiet and order reign in this shearing shed, built by my ancestors on Nulla Station in far south-western New South Wales. This scene is a far cry from the feverish activity and din that prevail here when the shearing is in full swing. Nulla shed, which can accommodate twenty-three shearers at any one time, is one of the largest shearing sheds in the region. Working at furious speed, these highly skilled operators fleece the sheep as they are brought up from the holding pens underneath.

Left: Culling sheep in Victoria's Strzelecki Ranges.

Left: Wilson's Promontory, the great granite tailpiece that juts out into Bass Strait at the far south-east of the continent, is regularly lashed by violent storms. Around the promontory are a number of peaceful inlets that offer shelter from the fury of the elements. Near the south-western tip is Oberon Bay, pictured here as the first rays of sunlight tint the sky and waters with delicate mauves and pinks.

Overleaf: The ancient towering dolerite peaks of Cradle Mountain, in Tasmania's Cradle Mountain-Lake St Clair National Park, are like a rock to cling to in rapidly changing times. The crystal clear, icy waters of the Twisted Lakes that nestle below the mountain provide welcome refreshment for many an exhausted hiker.

A piece of dead tumbleweed is blown across the Mertenalli sand dunes, near Wentworth in far south-western New South Wales. These shifting and wind-dominated dunes are part of Kelso Station and sit incongruously in the middle of extensive grazing lands.

As the sun gathers strength, stunted and broken eucalypts emerge from the early morning mists to reveal these desolate-looking grazing paddocks near Braidwood in south-eastern New South Wales.

The gathering light of dawn highlights the spectral shape of a dead eucalypt and
reveals sheep grazing unobtrusively amongst the tall grasses of this paddock near
Braidwood.

Right: Tree ferns and blackwood trees, distinguishable by the dark wood of their trunks and branches and the deep green of their foliage, are prominent among the vegetation in this valley in Victoria's Tarra-Bulga National Park. A recent shower of rain has freshened the foliage and intensified the richness of its verdure.

Overleaf: Only the hardiest of plants can survive the harsh, arid environment of the Mertenalli sand dunes, near Wentworth in south-western New South Wales.

The characteristic lichen-stained granite rocks of Wilson's Promontory and the rugged heath vegetation that covers much of its surface are both in evidence in this uncharacteristically calm scene at the very southern tip of the promontory. The lighthouse that stands as a warning sentinel on this point is obscured by the angle of the photograph.

Above: Steve Chambers, a West Australian wheat farmer, on his property Yoorooga.

Right: The early morning sun picks out the warm brownish hues in the historic iron shearing shed at Kelso Station in the far south-west of New South Wales. A recent storm has removed part of its roof. Beyond the pens is the Darling River, along which, in the days before road and rail transport came to the fore, the wool was transported to markets on barges towed by paddle steamers.

Overleaf: The waves break gently on the sands of Shell Beach, in the Innes National Park, at the south-west corner of South Australia's Yorke Peninsula. As it is off the main highways out of Adelaide, Yorke Peninsula is often bypassed by visitors to this part of the continent. Its praises are, therefore, rarely sung, and its beauties largely unappreciated.

The rich browns in the bark and trunks of these stately river gums, on the banks of the Darling River in south-western New South Wales, glow warmly in the sunlight. These beautiful trees line the banks of many of Australia's inland rivers, blending with the dominant shades of the landscape. Unfortunately many of those along the Murray River have succumbed to the high salinity which now afflicts that great stream. They survive, but with most of the colour bleached out of them they are but pale imitations of such hardy specimens as these.

Above: The Uniting Church at Penguin on the north coast of Tasmania.

Right: A boatshed on the shores of Dove Lake, high in Tasmania's central highlands, is the only sign of human intrusion into this largely inaccessible wilderness. To the south the twin peaks of Cradle Mountain, which soar to 1545 metres (5069 feet) above sea level, tower above this lake, one of the most picturesque of the numerous lakes, hewn out by ancient glaciers, that adorn this alpine region.

Left: Silhouetted against the light of a heavenly furnace, these late swimmers, at Seacliff Beach near Adelaide on the Gulf of St Vincent, linger in the surf. This suburban scene has been transformed into a place of resplendent beauty by the valedictory glow of the setting sun.

Overleaf: The cascading waters of Liffey Falls, in the Liffey Forest Reserve in northern Tasmania, tumble over dark rocks, illuminating the sombre greens of this secluded setting with a flash of brilliant white.

Above: A farmer in the Flowerdale Valley, near Boat Harbour in northern Tasmania.

Right: A time-ravaged gum arches one of its limbs over this bush track in the Flinders Ranges, the ancient and weathered mountains which, from a point about 200 kilometres (125 miles) north of Adelaide, sweep more than 400 kilometres (250 miles) northwards into the arid centre of the continent.

Left: Looking south from an elevated vantage point, the Freycinet Peninsula seems to dangle like a pendant from Tasmania's east coast. The sheltered inlet on the left is Wineglass Bay, which sweeps around towards Cape Forestier at the extreme left. Towards the right Mount Freycinet towers more than 600 metres (2000 feet) above sea level.

Overleaf: The pink-mauve clouds, painted by the rising sun, are palely reflected in the placid waters of Oberon Bay on the western side of Wilson's Promontory, the southernmost tip of the continent.

PHOTOGRAPHIC NOTES

This section is for those who want to know more about the technical aspects of photography. My approach to any photographic project is to keep everything as simple as possible. I surround myself with the best people in their respective fields. This allows me to get on with the job of taking images; if there is something wrong with the end product, then it is usually my fault.

Like any major undertaking, a photographic expedition involves many areas of specialization. No one can expect to make their own film, process it, maintain and organize cars and camping gear, and still find the time to take great photos.

EQUIPMENT

I use different cameras for different purposes and in different situations. They are outlined below.

The Fuji 617 is an excellent large-format panorama camera which is very user-friendly. It has a fixed 105 mm lens and takes four shots to a roll of 120 mm film.

Linhof's Technorama has a very sharp lens but is antiquated in body design when compared with its Fuji counterpart. Again, it takes four shots to the roll on 120 mm film with a fixed 90 mm lens.

I still love the Widelux F7 and F8 because of their portability. They achieve the panorama format by means of a 140 degree angle. Limited speed settings (only

⅟₁₅th, ⅟₁₂₅th and ½₅₀th second) make these cameras difficult to use in low-light situations, and some of the newer F8 cameras have problems with scanning and lenses—so beware; test before you buy!

Because the Widelux is totally mechanical, each camera needs servicing after 200 rolls to avoid vertical streaking. Some photographers complain about this, but it's a necessity with these cameras. Don't buy one if you are not prepared to service it regularly. They take 35 mm film and give 21 shots to a roll of 36 exposures. The viewfinder is inaccurate, so you have to judge just what the camera sees.

The Widelux 1500 Superwide is similar in features and design to the smaller format F7 and F8, except that it utilizes a 50 mm lens which can focused. It takes 120 mm film and delivers six frames to the roll. As the name suggests, the angle of view is 150 degrees, but the depth of field is not good. This is a difficult camera to use when foreground interest is critical. Available speeds are ⅛th, ⅟₆₀th and ½₅₀th second.

The trusty Nikon F4 is my preferred 35 mm camera. It is so simple to use in comparison with the panorama cameras.

My light meter is a Gossen Lunasix 111 with spot attachment. This is a simple meter which works well and has proved extremely reliable. I've seen all the fancy electronic meters but still prefer my old faithfuls. They have survived many knocks, bumps, and even swimming

lessons (not that I advise this kind of treatment).

When I need a tripod, I reach for the Linhof with ball-and-socket head. I have quick grip mounts on all cameras for speed of set-up. When you are out in the bush chasing good light, seconds wasted in fiddling with a tripod can mean missing a shot.

Finally, a word about my vehicle. Toyota—that's the word! As far as I'm concerned there is no better vehicle for off-road work in Australia. I have owned two troop carriers and travelled well over 300 000 kilometres (185 000 miles) in them. Toyotas are tough and reliable, which is very important in the outback, where a breakdown can mean at best a very long walk, and at worst a life-threatening situation.

FILM

I have been using Fuji film constantly for more than seven years. When it comes to shooting in natural light, it is the only logical choice. Fujichrome captures the whole spectrum of colours, from rich greens, blues, reds and yellows to the soft pastels of a sunrise or sunset. Australian greens, in particular, can be very subtle—for example, the many greens in eucalypt foliage—and on other kinds of film they can turn brownish.

The other advantage of Fuji film is the tight grain structure, which allows better definition. I almost always shoot on

transparency film—RFP 50 ASA and RDP 100 ASA—and I have recently had great results with the new Velvia, which simply leaves everything else for dead.

PROCESSING

Vision Graphics (Sydney) is the only choice for processing your hard-won images. They specialize in processing professional transparency film and no doubt process more than any other lab in Australia. I send film from all over Australia, and it's important to be able to get fast, intelligent feedback on your results, just in case you have a faulty camera or some other equipment problem. I would like to pay a special tribute to the people at Vision Graphics—Alan, Richard, Mark and Scott—who, over the years, have always given me that valuable feedback.

COURIERS

In all the years I have been freighting film, cameras and valuable transparencies right around the nation, I have never lost a parcel, thanks to TNT Couriers. Their service has been unbelievable. On one occasion, for example, I sent a parcel of exposed film from Marble Bar (a small, very remote town in outback Western Australia) for processing at Vision Graphics in Sydney, and the processed film was returned to me two days after I sent it!

INDEX

Note: Page numbers refer to references in text and captions.

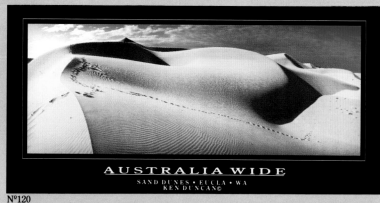

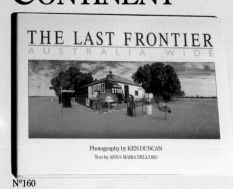